Fireflies

Words and Music by Adam Young
harp arrangement by Sylvia Woods

Moderately, with a groove

You would not be-lieve your eyes   if ten mil-lion fire – flies   lit up the world as I fell a –

sleep.   'Cause they'd fill the o – pen air   and leave tear-drops ev-'ry-where. You'd think

me rude,   but I would just stand and   stare.   I'd like to make my-self be-lieve

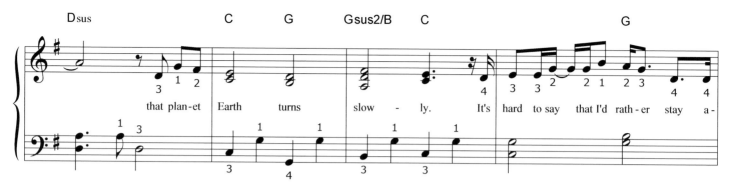

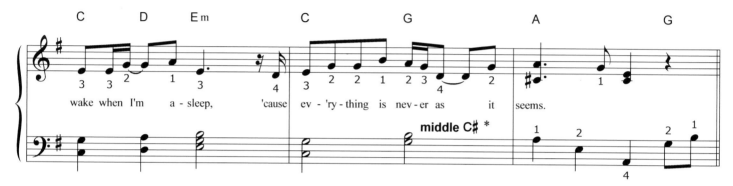

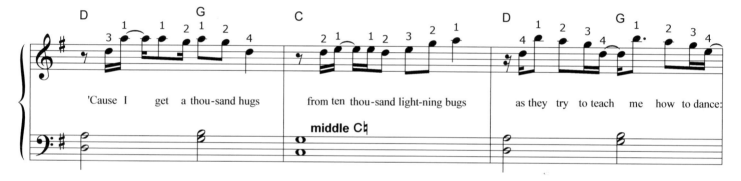

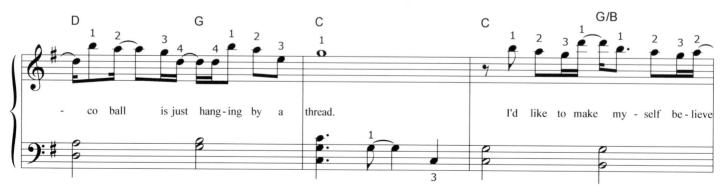

*This lever change may be omitted. If so, leave out both middle C# notes in the next measure, and omit the 2nd lever change.

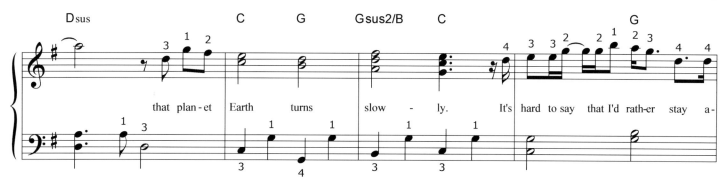

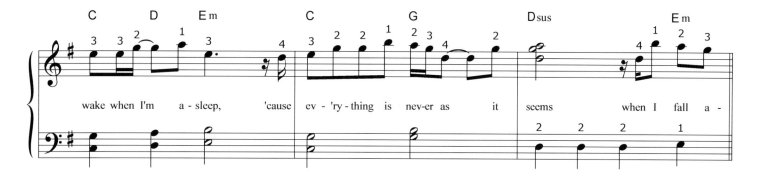

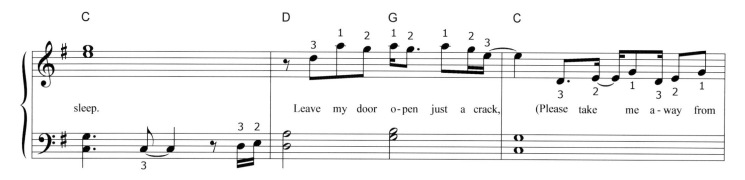

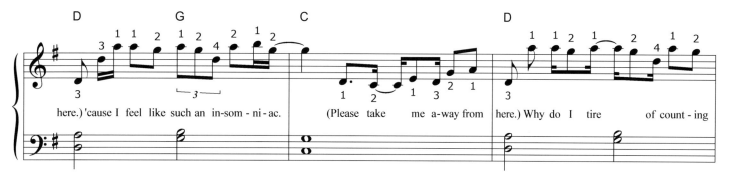

4

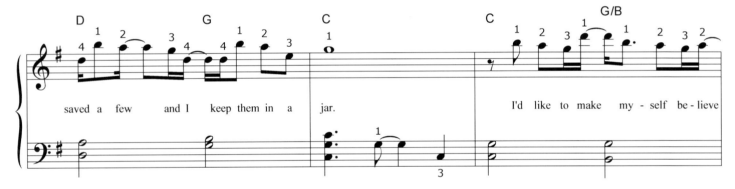

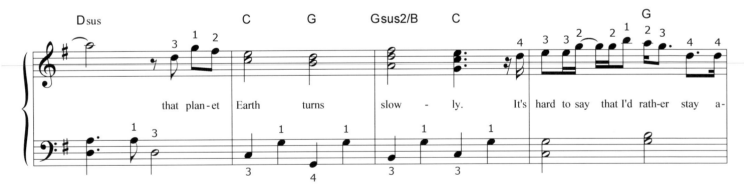